Hurtling Through Time and Space

A Field Trip for the Soul

Betty K. James

Cricket Cottage Publishing

Copyright © 2014 All rights reserved. No part of this work may be reproduced or transmitted in any form or by any means, electronic or otherwise, including photocopying and recording, or by any information storage or retrieval system, except as may be expressly permitted by the 1976 Copyright Act or in writing by the publisher.

Copyright 2014 Cricket Cottage Publishing. All rights reserved, Printed in the United States of America. Excerpts as permitted under the United States Act of 1976, no part of the publication may be reproduced or distributed in any form or by any means, or stored in a database or retrieval system, without the prior written permission of the publisher.

For information about group sales and permission, contact Cricket Cottage Publishing, LLC, 4409 Hoffner Avenue, Suite 127, Orlando, Florida 32812 or call 407-255-7785.

Website address: www.thecricketpublishing.com

Design: Peggy Magar
Cover Photo: Lindsay Magar
Editor: Peggy Magar

ISBN: 0692321527
ISBN-13: 978-0692321522

Hurtling Through Time and Space...A Field Trip For The Soul

What if being here on earth is a "field trip" for our soul's education?

Remember how exciting a field trip was when we were in school? We got to go someplace we'd not been, maybe eat food we'd never had? No sitting at a desk, no regular routine to follow? Someone new would lead us along, seeing, doing, hearing things different than "regular".

This day was different from beginning to end and we got to learn in a different environment. We got to try different things. Often we got to choose what we would do, try A or try B, and it didn't matter which you chose because it was all a part of the learning, and there was no wrong answer.

Now, wonder if the life you are living is your choice?
You wanted to try it out - being part human and part spirit a two-for-one kind of deal.
What would you do differently?
What would you choose to learn or do?
How excited would you be to be in a different "classroom"?

Life is a journey for our soul's growth - will you open the gate and experience life at 100%?

When you are ready, relish your field trip for all its possibilities and come join me on my journey.

Betty

I would love to hear from you. Contact me at:

Betty@FieldTripForTheSoul.com or
www.FieldTripForTheSoul.com

All photographs and artwork are copyrighted and contributed by Lindsay Magar, Betty James and Peggy Magar unless otherwise noted.

Dedication

How do I capture 70+ years of gratitude? What I know is my husband, daughter and son have been my greatest teachers.

I love you each beyond measure.

Also, I must include a special tribute to my friend Alexandra whose creative energy has been the foundation of the Goddess Gatherings in Gainesville and Orlando. This amazing group of women meet monthly for a "personal growth happy hour" where simply being women is more than enough. We laugh, talk and are real with each other. Each of you are the sisters I never had and mentors I cherish.

I am humbled by creation's gift of allowing me to find my way and the gift of sharing it with those who are interested. The muses use me as a vehicle each time I put pen to paper and soul appears there. I am grateful beyond measure for the opportunity to be me in this time, in this space. Namaste'

Categories

Aging and Transition
- Acceptance 8
- Life 17
- Aunt Ruth 18
- All I can do 21
- Which direction is the right direction 23
- Alone 32
- A good night's sleep 34
- My past 38
- Ryan 44
- Travel companion 46
- One day at a time 48
- Hiding me 51
- Morphing 65
- A black hole 67
- Day is done 70
- Mom's gone 90

Earth and Spirituality
- Field of green 4
- Knowing 13
- A monk's singing bowl 19
- Pelicans 22
- I believe 24
- Captain of my ship 25
- Seen or unseen 27
- Days fly by 29
- Ticking clock 33
- Gratitude 36
- Onions 41
- Where does sound end? 42
- My choice 43
- Soaring on wings 45
- By the sea 50
- Here today 52
- Am I old yet? 53
- Being here 54
- Should-ing on myself 55

- Light and shadow 57
- Gray day 59
- Time 64
- My part in the universe 68
- In the past 72
- Day of water 79
- Love 82
- Places to go and people to see 84
- Heart shaped shells 89
- Foam 91
- Infinite grace 92
- Good enough 93

Our family has served in many branches of the United States military during the last 150 years.

On behalf of our family, I thank the men and women who currently serve and those who have honorably served in the United States military.

To the families who love and support our military members, I am humbled by you.

Our nation is stronger because of every one of you.

Family and Friends

- I already know you 7
- My granddaughter 11
- Sea 12
- Every five minutes 14
- Things 15
- I'll be there 16
- Princess Peggy 20
- My mom 26
- Ode to my friends 28
- Old scripts 30
- Straight lines 35
- A new phone 37
- Friendship 39
- Homecoming 47
- Goddesses gather 49
- A new day 66
- Goddesses are we all 69
- Looking back 71
- Mommom 73
- Marriage glue 74
- A new life 77
- Sauter's farm 78
- Dear baby 81
- Christmas stockings 86
- Truths 87
- Any name will do 88

Military

- Traveling with pop 10
- Do you see me? 56
- My flag 61
- The USAF dad 62
- Earthbound 76
- A veteran's way 85
- The brothers' bond 94

Passion

- Furious love 6
- Ageless love 31
- Trying to nap 40
- A space of my own 63
- On the road 75
- Young love 80

Family of Fur

- Little Bit 9
- A small glimpse 58
- Our feral cat 60
- A family of mutts 83

About the Author 97
List of Poems by Name 98
List of Poems by Page Number 99

This emblam was specifically designed by daughter, friend, and military spouse, Peggy Magar, and holds the following:

- our declaration of support for every branch of the military and members both past and present;
- the name of every branch of the military;
- a picture of the flag we fly in our yard every day;
- "Semper Paratus" which is the Coast Guard's motto. Semper Paratus translates to, "Always Ready" which exemplifies all branches of our military family; and
- the gold ribbon which we will display until all military members are home from every war and conflict including those missing in action (MIA).

Field of green

a little blade of grass
lost in a field of green
I think of you and me,
are we ever really seen?

a grain of sand
in the desert wide
do I count?
the speck cried

a bright star
far in the sky
am I a dream
or do I fly?

each of us a thread
in creations tapestry
constantly evolving
as God's reality

Furious love

lips of love
tongues on fire
raging hearts
lusts desire

scattered clothes
skin entwined
primal moves
a feast Divine

quieted storms
satisfaction complete
'til love again
fuels loves' heat

I already know you

unborn baby
tiny and dear
i already see you
very clear

tiny hands and feet
a crystal tear
trusting in life
you dispel any fear

the angels whisper
in your ear
telling you secrets
we cannot hear

the cycles repeated
millions of times a year
but for this family
you bring heaven near

Little Bit

other cats have come and gone
yet you still hold on

Mikey was one, Scruffy two, next, Big Boy number three of this zoo
all of them passed on long before you

each of these pets i can see now
a different child fully loved somehow

total trust always there
we gave each other ultimate care

forever true an infinite grace
fully expressed in your furry face

each touched a place my spirit knows well
where love abides like an endless well

when you passed from here to there
my sadness mellowed because always i cared
for each creature i've come across - and
remembering you each gentles my loss

Traveling with pop

whenever i fly
i touch your face
among the clouds
in this high space

it's where i always find you
beyond the bounds of earth
our happy place, you and i
halfway to the heaven of our birth

perspectives change drastically
remembering your life's passion
one on earth – mom and we kids
the other time aloft that's rationed

earthly worries fall behind
physical life a very small piece
of all we are and can be
when life's passion we seize

My granddaughter

she is with me now
yet off on her own
we both find solace
in the ocean's home

a place to calm down
to reframe our life
understanding our value
even in strife

these two souls
together again
a place of refuge
through thick and thin

once we return to routine
we go our separate ways
knowing we're connected
every single day

so young and old
hold the world at bay
a little longer please
just one more day

Sea

without a past
where would i be
adrift in the moment
on the sea?

the past is my teacher
both fair and foul
coloring each day
with a whisper or growl

Knowing

knowing that love is all there is
gives me a reason to live

eyes and ears, hands and feet
honor the grace of being complete

returning to God with a joyous song
discovery and beauty a life lived strong

how do i know what's best for me?
is this what i want God to see?

when every word, act or deed
comes from love; i'll succeed

then i rest easy knowing i'm done
mission accomplished my spirit has won

when i turn to the unknown
a glimpse brings me home

we are all of God in different forms
knowing each other before we're born

now i'm back to spirit alone
as before earth was my home

my soul lifts to all that is
beside God's love i truly live

Every five minutes

i am so sorry
you have to pee
every five minutes
at least it seems to be

sleeping on your back
is a thing of the past
but you know
that won't last

in the name of a babe
your body's not your own
but in three months
you'll bring her home

i guess nana's
are here to provide
support and reassurance
for a new parent's ride

into the life
that's totally new
you are now a family
it'll never be just you

Things

So why do old pictures evoke wanting the "things" that are already gone? Am I missing my mom or an aunt to whom they belonged? Do I long for the times that are passed? Or am I just greedy and want it all?

I feel drawn to the past . . . I loved our big living room with blue velvet couch, dining room table, clear ginger jar lamps. Family gathered round, Mom, Pop, cousins and aunts. Our own are children growing and happy with so much going on. Bud and I are hanging on – not to each other but to the flurry of life itself. Our home was full of people, movement, love, laughter, tears, anger – lots of growth everywhere.

Now in the quiet of daily life, what a gift it would be if the walls could bring back the sounds of those times. However, our memories will serve us as we dip into that well of when we lived more fully than words can tell.

I'll be there

your momma's belly jumps
as you stretch for room
i'm missing it all
i fuss and fume!

as soon as i can
i will be there
bringing this love
i want to share

Life

life moves onward
regardless of the day
sorrow and joy
part of our play

accepting fully
to **be** is the key
we move with grace
or rigidity

the choice remains
moment by moment
we wrestle with our life
living in grace or choosing torment

the wisest decision
i make each day
is living with joy
then giving some away

Aunt Ruth

My Aunt Ruth is gone her time here done;
she's moved on in the light of the Son.

But oh! How I remember the stories she told
the past came alive as they would unfold.

Strange sounding names of my heritage, my past
grandparents & cousins all too involved to grasp.

She was the historian keeping it all straight
who belonged to whom what was their fate.

Her generation is gone to a reunion in God's grace;
her love surrounds me as I see her smiling face.

My mom, her sister, is there with Grama Vesta and you -
seated in a garden with skies so blue.

The clouds are your chair and stars are in your hair
each of you, a golden angel, floating on air.

My world has changed since Ruth has departed
the last one to give up she was the most softhearted.

Now our mom's are gone as we cousins share
the joy and sorrow of children who care.

I'll think of you, Aunt Ruth, down by the gate
enjoying the flowers as you patiently sit and wait.

A monk's singing bowl

the monk's singing bowl
reaches inside of me
the sounds take me deeper
into eternity

there i commune
with creations' guides
finding myself
without my pride

only a knowing
i'm in the right place
to receive full love
God touching my face

Princess Peggy

you are pregnant
it's easy to see
my darling daughter,
princess peggy

your simple life
is terribly askew
you're now carrying
a life that's new

it's a grand time
for rich and you
to create your own
marriage glue

but i'll miss
being with you two
loving you both
and the baby that's due

the life you know
will change overnight
when baby comes home
to his birthright

take care of each other
as i know you do
remembering always
i love each of you

All I can do

all i can do
is what's right for me
not pressure others
into the path i see

    for each road taken
    adds to the tapestry
    woven with care
    creating our reality

        i work to stay aware
        of what's right & true
        for me . . .
        not you

            is my path important?
            my guess is yes & no
            for it simply enriches
            what God already knows

                all i have to offer
                for creations gift
                is my own perspective
                that times' tide is swift

                    so i'll do it today
                    whatever it is
                    for only then
                    do i glimpse my bliss

Pelicans

they fly in a line
the leader's wings beat
each of the followers
help propel the fleet

each takes a turn
to follow or lead
no matter the position
they keep a steady speed

could this be an example
for humanity's quest?
letting go of our ego
letting it take a rest

we're all in this together
none of us are alone
to be at peace with ourselves
to find our way home

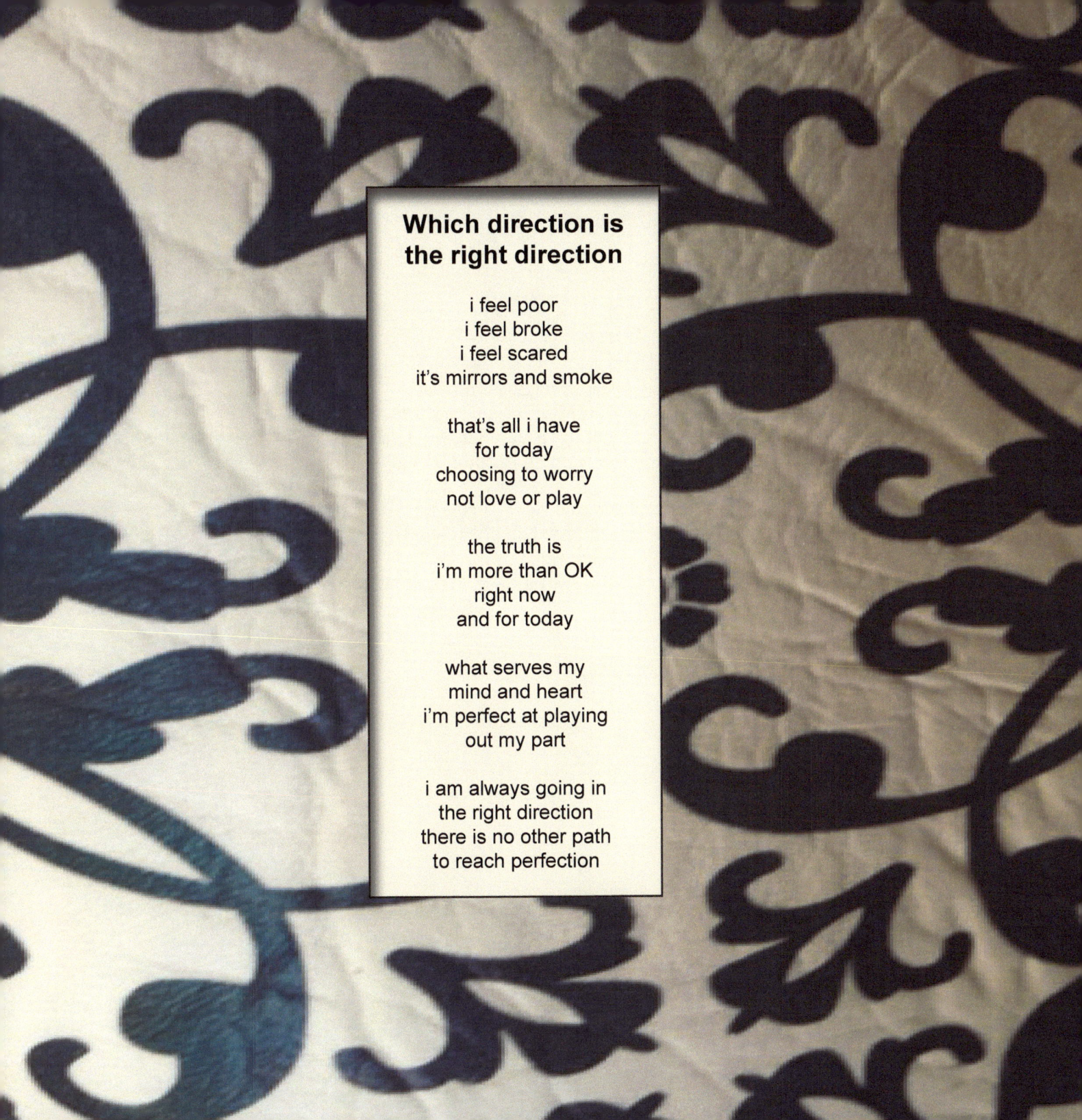

Which direction is the right direction

i feel poor
i feel broke
i feel scared
it's mirrors and smoke

that's all i have
for today
choosing to worry
not love or play

the truth is
i'm more than OK
right now
and for today

what serves my
mind and heart
i'm perfect at playing
out my part

i am always going in
the right direction
there is no other path
to reach perfection

I believe

Surrender	=	being open to all possibilities
Courage	=	believing in what I know but cannot see
Knowing	=	I am valuable to God and the Universe even when it's hard to do
Peace	=	I am always going in the right direction
Truth	=	each one of us is doing the best we know in any given moment
Gratitude	=	that I see and hear through my heart
Amazed	=	at the wonder of life, the earth, the cosmos
Strength	=	self-awareness
Christmas	=	every babe that's ever born is celebrated this holy morn

Captain of my ship

a to z
and everything between
what outlasts
is what's unseen

for bodies come
and bodies go
but spirit remains
a steady glow

it's what leads the way
to unknown realms
for as captain of my ship
i am at the helm

straight and true
or ziggity zag
life ends folded in spirit
as exhausted we sag

to rejuvenate
i head out again
each new day
i eagerly begin

My mom

before my mother passed away
we talked of life, death and such
what she said she'd miss the most
was simply reaching out to touch

it broke my heart
i felt the same
i'd miss her touch
more than i could explain

i thought real hard
and asked for grace
to take us from
this hurting place

now whenever someone
touches me with love
i'll know it's her
reaching from above

Seen or unseen

the rain falls
plants and trees rejoice
the soothing touch
of something moist

is this the elixir
of life itself
to truly be touched
understanding what's felt

soft and gentle
hard and cruel
nothing bad
and nary a rule

how can we be free
and know it all
if we're afraid
to slip and fall?

so the game is played
to look really good
instead of living
with NO "shoulds"

each day allows
us to the gather
the gifts of our life
that really matter

Ode to my friends

i know it's happened many times
when my heart is open wide
allowing my soul to shine
by inviting others inside

the door again open
we're off on a lark
of love and light
shutting out the dark

two souls cavorting
through the uncharted sea
sharing their joys
carefree as you please

Days fly by

this is how
days go by
always moving
they swiftly fly

with joy and faith
we take them in
then tomorrow
we begin again

Old scripts

how to let go
of my old script
when someone i love
is stuck in a pit?

i firmly believe
we choose our life
learning and teaching
in ease and strife

life can be grand
or hellish it's true
why do some choose
chaos' brew?

all i can do
is check in today
appreciating all choices
to see love always & all ways

for as i get centered
my heart expands
with gratitude and joy
as you hold my hand

no matter my dear
where each life goes
we travel beyond here
to love's gracious glow

Ageless love

when we make love
  it's different today
    the young lovers of yore
      are a thought form away

  we tussle and rustle
    are intense and laugh
      tying our lover's knot
        then take a bath

      it doesn't matter
        morning noon or night
          we celebrate our love
            how and when it feels right

          a touch ... a smile
            working side by side
              talking or silent
                there's nothing to hide

              through young love
                maturity and age
                  marriage and children
                    love's magnificent at any stage

Alone

holding on
  day by day
    i can't live with you but
      without you is a price i won't pay

the decades have shown
it's the marriage glue
never letting go of the power
of just we two

how will i make it
  through today
    alone, alone
      keeping pain at bay

      one of us gone
        equals a broken soul
          afraid of the future
            and what it will hold

        doesn't matter
      which one is first
    alone the other cannot
quench loves thirst

  please understand my love
that the one left behind
will keep loves' faith
that we'll be together in time

Ticking clock

The special offer is available for only a short time. Time is ticking away and I can see that, "I have to act NOW!!!!"

Offers are for a specified period. If I want a "deal", I have only a certain time frame to get it. The questions are: What's really being offered? What's the guaranteed with all the fine print? What isn't covered? Is this really a "special" price? Can I get it for less later on? Can I afford the price to begin with?

What if my life is God's special offer for a limited time? When the offer expires, is it over – gone? What if life itself is what's being offered? Am I willing to pay the price? Is there a guarantee? For what? Do I have to live a certain way? What's in the fine print that I may not see?

I believe my Creator and I are a team. Once I agree to the contract and begin my life, God's part is done as I have been given total choice of how my life will be lived. That is my payment for this great "deal."

Will I choose to see and live in the beauty of water, leaves, sunshine, joy and love ... OR will I chose any of the other millions of ways other people live. Will I "see" the miracle of morning birds going about their day? Foraging and defending their territory and still they sing their song for the sheer joy of it.

For me, morning coffee is part of a day's beauty. Is there any better taste of a day's potential? Hot, steamy, creamy and sweet with a touch of bitterness? I swish it around in my mouth appreciating the mix of it all, waiting for the kick of caffeine to set in.

A good night's sleep

a good slumber
all night through
is a rare gift
and hard to do

my mind races
there are minor aches
a trip, maybe, three to pee
a full night's rest is at stake

youngster sleep hard
like a lump of lead
oldsters can greet night
with a sense of dread

Straight Lines

i am not fond of straight lines
bendy and curvy how my life's defined
no straight and narrow no box around me
i finally figured out being me is being FREE!

Gratitude

the days go by
so fast it seems
before i know it
the night brings dreams

so the years
blend and meld
while in your love
i'm safely held

it's hard to know where
i start and you end
this living unit is
where our lives blend

more life's behind us
then lay ahead
being together
nothing's to dread

gratitude for each day
we get to share the view
as we settle gently
into age's golden hue

A new phone

i love this phone
that takes me everywhere
i stay connected
inside-outside, i'm on the air

i love this phone
it's here to stay
no one knows where i am
they just hear what i say

i love this phone
that sings, talks and squeaks
it has a mind of its own
and when lost even speaks

i love this phone
given by a son so rare
now it answers with my name
from the yard, bath or easy chair

i love this phone
but even more
i love the son
who made our family four

My past

  i am surrounded by love's past
  Mom, Ruth and Jenny - heritage holds fast

a cup and saucer a diamond ring
shiny silver's twinkling bling

so these are the keepsakes lovingly displayed
to see and be seen every single day

their presence sits with me
as though i were on their knee

play patty cake, dress up or dolls
these women shaped a sense of my all

exact memories fade but the feelings remain
cherished with joy like bubbly champagne

their gentle love reaches beyond here
as i "see" each one and shed my tears

for we women give beyond time
to ensure that family is a tie that binds

Friendship

here i show up
just as i am
simple and plain
like pb and jam

the staple of life
is simple for me
love is the fuel
for my identity

this simple seed
with water and light
leads me forward
to my soul's delight

a silver box
tied with ribbon of gold
a gift immeasurable
of how our life will unfold

Trying to nap

mid-day sleepiness
i sometimes dread
as a wild roller coaster
blasts inside my head

words rhyming
touching my heart
when i truly want
my nap to start

Oh, but NOOOOOO
words rumble about
screaming "you can't sleep
now let me out"

"put me on paper
before i'm lost
your hands must work
because i am the boss"

forget the nap
take pen in hand
and enter creations
holy land

Onions

an onion has a brown covering
which is tough and scarred
protects the tender inside
so it can't be marred

in many ways our outer shell
is like an onion's too
protecting and coloring
everything we do

you and i can explore
the layers of who we are
the tears will flow freely
soothing an unhealed scar

deep inside is our tender self
a place of sweet peace
the truth of our existence
ours to access and to release

always keep reaching
for the core of you
cutting through old layers
finding love renewed

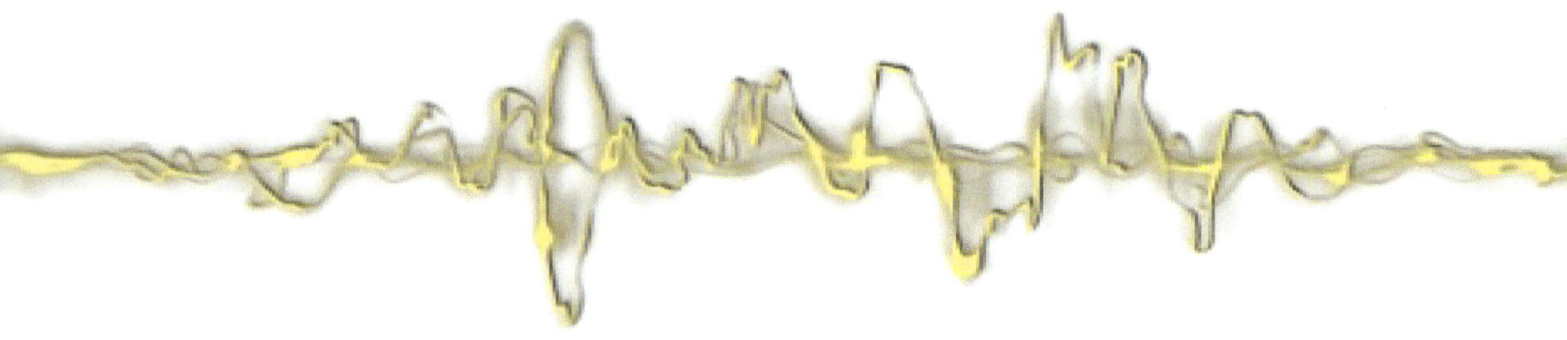

Where does sound end?

Off to a concert tonight with my daughter, granddaughter, neighbor, and a good friend.

I am totally open to the show, the sounds, voices, lights, words all shared with my loving group of women. The talent and heart of the women performers is truly amazing. Their voices praising love, God, home, family and yet again love. The joy they bring to their work and the audience is a gift for the soul.

My question posed is, "where and when do the sounds once created end?" They remain in my heart and head long after hearing them; still reverberating within me. The creation of endless vibrations of love, joy, and beauty are beyond the sounds alone.

What an impact they have on the universe one audience, one individual at a time.

My choice

the decision
for all to go well
laid the results
for all to go well

change happens
once the decision's made
today can be different
letting the past fade

there's a pivotal awareness
that i'm in charge
small decisions inside
equal results that are large

Ryan

the babe is gone
home to God
we don't know why
but onward we plod

for in my heart
i know it's true
he is as sad
as me and you

to be in your arms
was the a choice he made
that's all changed
in how life's played

yet we know
as we weep
in God's hands
is where he'll sleep

Soaring on wings

    i love it all
    candles, table and chair
    sunlight or fog
    here or there

        what is right now
        whatever it be
        is perfectly right
        just for me

            as i "see"
            from my heart
            God and i
            create my part

                the gift is knowing
                i get to choose
                now that i "get" it
                i can never loose

                      i'll soar on wings
                      living the moment
                      with gratitude for all
                      i embrace en – joy – ment

Travel companion

Cozy slippers protect me from the morning chill. So much to feel – this pen on the paper as it glides across the page creating words that spill from my soul. A cup of coffee, my hand on my face, a place to rest my chin and feel my breath warm, wispy and constant.

To truly taste, feel, see, smell and hear "life" is our greatest opportunity to live in gratitude.

What is the single factor that can move me from having only a physical life experience? Love is the answer for me. That one emotion moves me from my physical plane to a spiritual one. My life's goal then is to live my life through love, with love, tasting, smelling, hearing, feeling, and seeing love on my journey each day.

For me, during this lifetime, I chose love as my travel companion.

Homecoming

you're coming home
repeats in my head
to visit your folks
to sleep in your own bed

you're coming home
i can hardly wait
you're coming home
let's make a date

to sit by the sea
time to share
really being together
is all that I care

at this stage in life
you're not here or there
someplace in between
your life's in the air

i feel like i'm losing
this son of mine
a special bond
we're two of a kind

so carve out some time
for only you & me
something special – or not
i just want to be "we"

from the day you were born
'til away you drove
you've lived your life
however you chose

now when you join us
it's friend to friend
spreading zest and joy
cherishing family again

so drive safely
take no chances
hurry on home
where blue water dances

One day at a time

to be alone
without you near
is an abyss
of bottomless fear

i can't know
that's how it'll be
the futures not
mine to see

my abiding faith
will be there
and carry me
through times foul and fair

for right now-

it's time for bed
now snuggled to you
everything's just right
until our final adieu

Goddesses gather

once a month
is our cycle
we see each other
and we're kind of psycho

dressing silly
having wine
we eat well
getting lost in time

a place to express
our tender self
or let our hair down
like a mischievous elf

candles lit
we're each aware
the path to love
is to truly care

just us girls
acting out or not
we slowly weave
friendship's knot

carrying it home
sharing with others
broadening understanding
of our sisters and one another

By the sea

the infinity of life in sea and sky
which are seen by my mind's eye

why are so many people worldwide
drawn to these waters as their guide?

could it be a reminder to us
of our connection to universal playfulness?

i come to the sea in joyful repose
knowing I'll find poems to compose

it's taking the time to sit, to be still, working in the quiet
i let the waves wash gently over me, calming life's chaotic riot

endless sky, sea and sun bring me home
to how my soul's done

i see the true me peaceful and calm
my hands quickly tripping over sonnet and psalm

so many words that have to rhyme
exposing truths gently crafted over time

Hiding me

simply being short made me see
everyone looks down on me
that belief was seared upon my soul
i knew for sure i was less than whole

at a young age my eyes needed fixing
i survived the darkness, pain and stitching
i knew from then on my place and my role
would always be less than whole

perfection's the key, or so i was taught
never measuring up OR being quite whole
seeing my worth in a mirror is what i bought
and as a good daughter, i absorbed the role

oh how well i learned to hide
what was really going on inside
i had to be more to gain loves' goal
as i was obviously less than whole

by age 15, my pain was well hidden
when along came true love - quite unbidden
this was a guy who loved rock n' roll
he already saw me as beautiful and whole

tho' i was shorter by more than a foot
i knew this was where my life could take root
trembling and unsteady like a young foal
i felt the power of being almost whole

now beauty brings fullness to everyday life
i know i'm an excellent mother and wife
when i am quiet, spirit reminds me i'm whole
where life's a theater and i'm in control

Here today

my life is now mine
to create as I wish
sixty-six years invested
I chose bliss

here today
gone tomorrow
a life well lived
ends without sorrow

for rebirth's a choice
to try again
to love each day
to the very end

Am I old yet?

    am i old yet?
      how far will i go?
        a decade or two?
       fast or slow?

          am i old yet?
           as there's much to do
             i'll lap up the days
                whether many or few

              am i old yet?
            or as i die
                will i simply release
                  my soul to fly?

Being here

how fortunate
i am to live here
among luscious beauty
for many a year

i'm older now
youth left behind
appreciation and love
now fill my mind

Should-ing on myself

how do i know
where i fit
sometimes i wonder
if i should just sit

take my time
to feel what's right
settle down peacefully
quiet as night

my busy mind
is hard at work
leading me in circles
listing my quirks

i should on myself
from past to present
beaten down by the voice
that is incessant

i should
do laundry and every chore
i should
always do more

i call it the
"itty bitty shitty committee"
it has my own voice
it doesn't show any pity

for peace doesn't come
from beating myself up
but to drink from
loves' golden cup

Do you see me?

do you see me
as i stumble and fall?
hearing bombs
that aren't there at all

do you see me
standing tall
as the flag passes
different from you all?

do you see me
tattered and torn
reliving the hell
alone and forlorn?

do you see me
under a white cross
united again
with all the lost?

do you see me
by your side
reminding us all
of honors pride?

do you see me
in your carefree day
doing as you wish
as at rest i lay?

do you see me
hearing freedoms bell
the story's not over
the future you'll tell

Light and shadow

It takes light and physical form to create shadows.
Without "matter", light has no way to define itself.
We ARE the light in physical form.

We matter.

A small glimpse

    is this how creation
    carries on?
    each new one
    morphs from what's gone?

        an endless cycle
        the past giving birth
        to all that's new
        upon this earth?

            as we each
            lie down and die
            another will rise
            with a song and a sigh

                bringing their gifts
                to the stew
                that ends up being
                either me or you?

                    is that what they mean
                    when they say we're all one
                    blended and folded
                    from someone else's run?

                        or am i trying
                        to make sense
                        of the universe
                        from too small a glimpse?

Gray day

it's gray and chilly
clouds rushing in
making it perfect
to visit a friend

i stay in bed
under covers warm
a good book I read
as it thunders and storms

hot cocoa in a mug
grilled cheese beside
i really don't care
what goes on outside

i know for sure
tomorrow'll be nice
so for today
i give in to my vice

 **Our feral cat**

you began life hidden under a house
it was dark and safe quiet as a mouse

not the prettiest of the feral crew
but once you bit me i had to keep you

you love to sleep under the covers next to me
snuggly and sweet as could be

you love the dog more than any others
not people nor cats ... the dog is your brother

big lab, Jessie, gentle and calm
is your safe place a comfortable balm

your incessant meow is a command
to do your bidding whatever the demand

catching birds in mid-air
a warrior's heart killing without care

now you're old, scared, deaf and slow
hiding under a bed the only safety you know

forever more i'll hear your call
and in my heart you're still soft and small

My flag

Red, white and blue
my flag waves proud
speaking my allegiance
outside – out loud

The USAF dad

puffy clouds billowing high
i'm among them when i fly

an unknown landscape as far as i can see
and yet i'm home, gratefully

only blue sky over my head
an unfettered place as my life's re-read

why when i'm here do i tend to stew
from where i sit, my life's in review

i know when i land i'll start anew
i am different having loved you

i can see his flight suit and sob my good-byes
watching him take off charging upward off he'd fly

his destiny beckoned among the clouds
as his family at home made him proud

so we'd wait 'til he blew in
as fresh and strong as a clearing wind

all smiles and laughter high on life, still
his heart's hung here with his children and wife

A space of my own

What would I do with a space of my own?
Where creative juices flow and have room to grow?

What would I do all by myself?
Be wise and strong or a grumpy elf?

It's never a place I've been before
an unlimited me that I could explore

Poetry and collages to name a few
so much to try - wonder what I CAN do?

Will I be too old if I got the chance
or be beaten down by life's jaded dance?

For so many years, I've put this aside
now there's hope for this artist to ride.

Time

i pull the sands
of time to me
counting and measuring
how to be

missing completely
a vista divine
creation sits beside me
endless as time

the poems are
more than i am
pulling me forward
as only God can

Morphing

a girl child
changes and grows
in tiny steps
her life flows

barely noticed
by family and friends
the path once started
never ends

for we morph
into who we are
ever reaching
for "our" star

A new day

a new day
a new name
life will never
be the same

you were a child yesterday
you're a mother today
the rest of life is held at bay
as this tiny seed holds sway

your body's not
yours alone
but shared with a babe
until it's born

now your life
revolves around him
tho' not even here
the changes begin

A black hole

the fear looms large
like a gaping black hole
that soon you'll be gone
and i'll cease to be whole

life as i know it
surrounded by pain
so great is my loss
i'll never be me again

these medical crisis
tear me apart
i will cease living
with the stop of your heart

i know we're connected
through time and space
but i cannot comprehend
never again touching your face

My part in the universe

What if we are a cooperative venture with God? How do I understand my place in such a venture? Are the experiences of this small dot of humanity really, truly valuable? How do I put my head around that?

My willingness to co-operate ... or not ... is the doorway to seeing myself.

Goddesses are we all

goddesses gather
12 times a year
a personal growth
happy hour is why we're here

listen a moment
to all our chatter
serious or funny
it doesn't even matter

for what's happening
is what we women do
being with each other
is friendships glue

there is much more
but you get my drift
we listen and share
each of us a valued gift

none of us the same
except from within
life's playing field
is under our skin

times can be good
times can be bad
the difference can be found
in the friends we've had

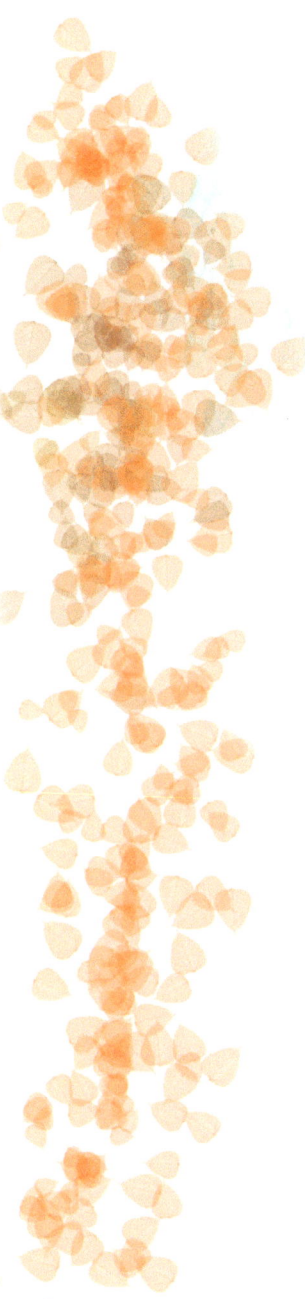

Day is done

day is done
and so am i
outside is dark
as deeply i sigh

my head on a pillow
feet propped high
lights turned off
rest is nigh

Looking back

my little guy
smiles abound
always busy
rarely a frown

how the years
tumble past
together you and i
always had a blast

water fights
sliding in mud
running free
really good buds

as your world expands
i'm left in the shadows
watching your star rise
my love feels fallow

In the past

i used to need
to be *in* the sea
catching enormous waves
challenging myself constantly

those days are past
now i "see" the sea
a consistent reminder
of eternity

in the past power was success
conquering obstacles the decree
now i sit in wonder
beside the sea

representing life
in all its forms
there's a peace for me
of coming home

Mommom

i wish you could
come sit with me
tell how you felt
as i carried my first baby

were you scared
of all that could go wrong?
Were you proud
of how i was strong?

when the baby was born
what did you think
knowing that i
was on the brink

of discovering the world
only a mother knows
of dishes and diapers
and a runny nose

so how did you react
when you heard the news
that your very own baby
was putting on your shoes?

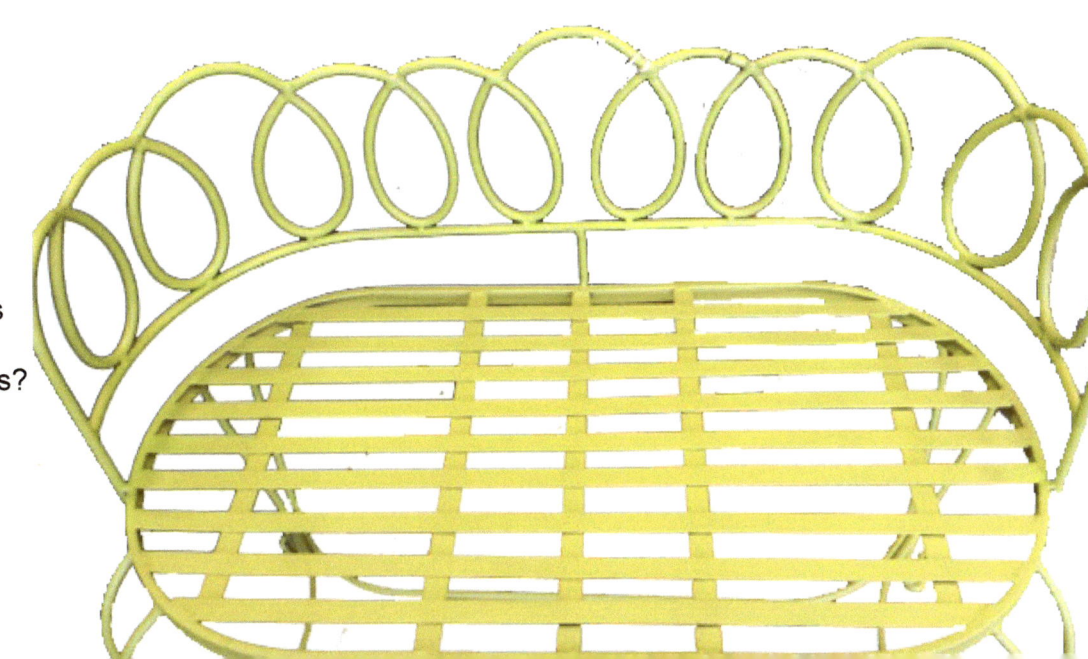

Marriage glue

i love my Bud
i love who i am
i love our life
we are happy as clams

it is simple
it is true
it is our
marriage glue

On the road

i love my car
it isn't much
but gets me around
on errands and such

it's old fashioned
a bit tattered and worn
like me it's traveled
through every life storm

we're not perfect it's true
i take time and get a clue
it's not what's inside
but how i see the view

in the moment
lose or win
each is a gift
to see within

silly laughter
tears of pain
accepting it all
i alone do gain

do i hold
my desires at bay
or does my soul
dance and play

just roll down the windows
open the top
just happy for me
i don't want to stop

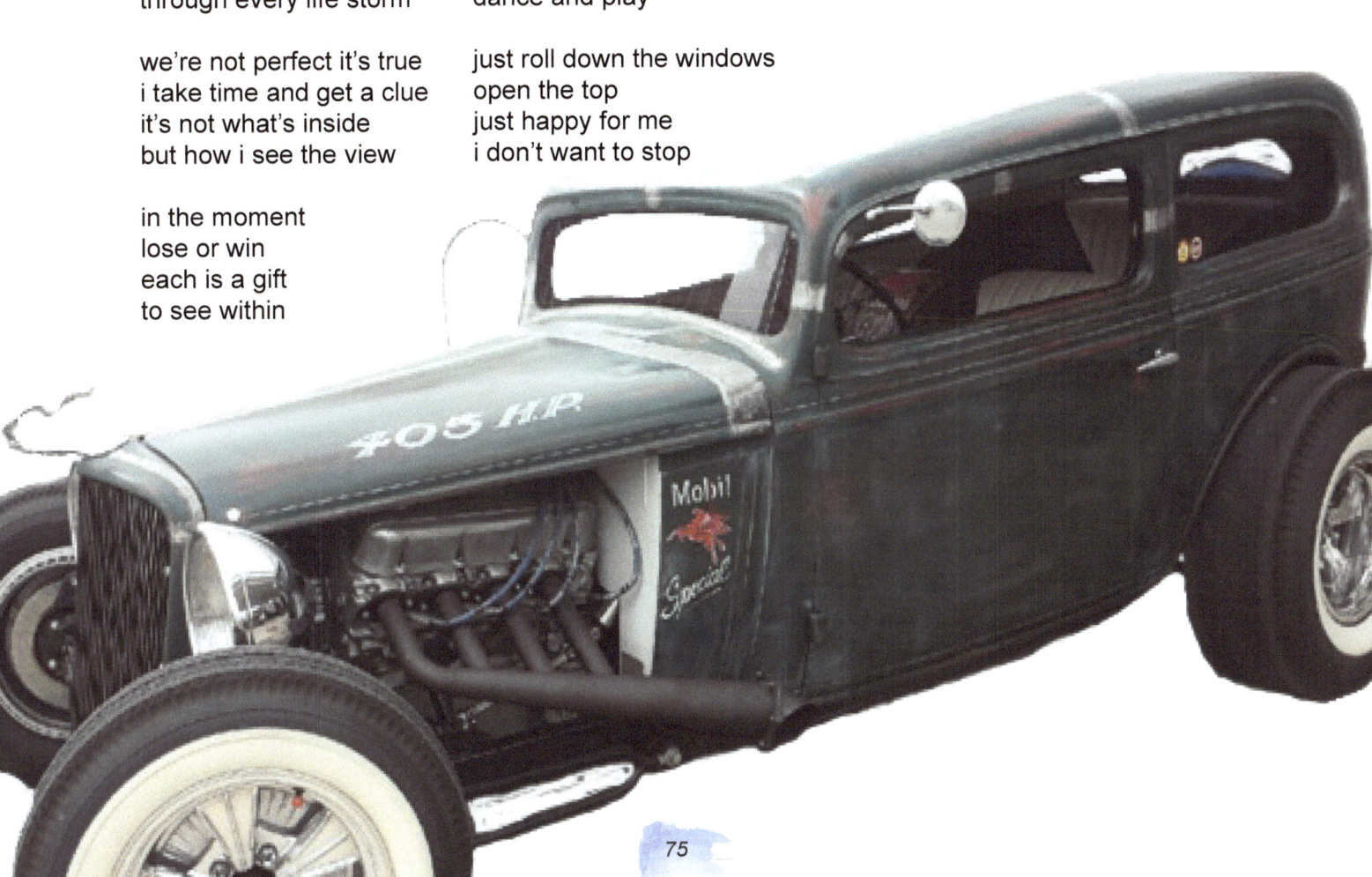

Earthbound

wings of silver
wings of gold
a million stories
left untold

the pilots are dead
or their minds soft
never again
to go aloft

what we've lost
is the vision true
that America's freedom
has passed to me and to you

A new life

my baby's having a baby
a miracle to be sure
physical proof
that love endures

i love this baby
tho' yet unborn
expectantly awaited
as the coming morn

once you're here
you'll light our lives
as sure as
the sun will rise

your sweet face
will show the way
with joy and beauty
for all of our days

i'll hold your hand
and watch you grow
let you teach me
what I need to know

in your newness
is divine light
it also shows me
my birthright

Sauter's farm

I remember the Sauter's whenever I've seen
farmland spread out fertile and green.

Theirs was the oldest homestead Nebraska ever had
bequeathed from Lincoln to their great-grand dad.

For more than 100 years they gave this huge spread
their blood sweat and tears as farmers they were bred.

Their ancient farm had a garden too
where in the spring a gnarled red bud tree grew.

Against winter's stark world the redbud would bloom
each branch a colorful arc defying the land's gloom.

They gave so much to the new neighbors or' the field
a living history, a family connection as many lonely hearts healed.

What I remember from years ago at 90 Bill gave up farming;
Sofia's arthritis crippled her up while Alma, the oldest, was still charming.

Slowly one by one their time on earth
was over and done, gone was a simple worth.

Over the years, we've lost track. None are still living but,
in our memories the Sauter's farm keeps giving.

Day of water

mists hang low
over lake and land
filling earth's pores
with a gentle hand

so it touches
my face and hair
like diamond dust
from my creator's care

gratitude here and gone
like a whispered prayer
not forgotten by me
but sent to ether's air

Young love

your soft breath
brushes my face
as you gently fold me
into your embrace

this is where
i long to be
when i pass
into eternity

so it's been
from the start
one great love
within two hearts

Dear baby

dear baby
you're so far away
yet you're in my thoughts
each and every day

you're growing so big
and you're still inside
where your mommy keeps you safe
and you can enjoy the ride

floating and stretching
first a finger then a hand
soon your space
will be a constricting band

you'll want out
to play and grow
as I wonder
what seeds you'll sow

for now take your time
enjoy being inside
where creation's journey
does reside

Love

I never know where the words will lead me; but generally, it is back to knowing that:

#1 Life is good
#2 I choose to be here now
#3 The vital energy for everything is Love/God/Spirit/All that Is/the Universe/Creation.

Every plant, drip of water, sunrise, or feather is part of me and I get to choose what I do with that information. I may get lost in all the "stuff" of life, but, my core belief is – LOVE IS ALL THERE IS.

A family of mutts

no pedigrees here
mutts are we all
but we each heard
true love's call

a family is formed
cats, dogs and me and you
all strays brought in
creating loves glue

one from hurricane Katrina
one in South Dakota boots
three from Orlando
the last with no roots

a motley crew
of fangs and fun
a joyous journey
under the Florida sun

through it all
the tie that will bind
is the love
that we all find

i'm done for the night
easing into sleep
the world is right
with pets to keep – safe

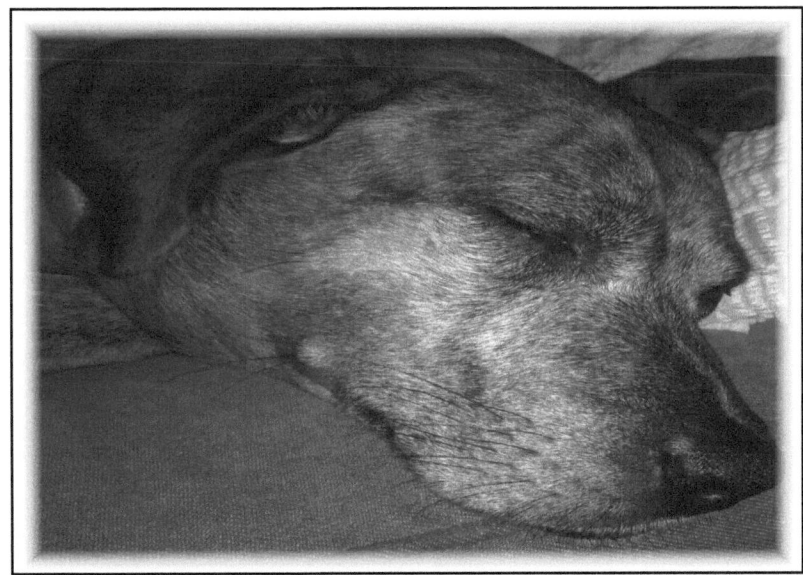

Places to go and people to see

there's so much world i want to see
far away and exotic - a yearning inside of me

i'll bond with someone i've yet to meet
we'll connect in a heartbeat

knowing each other from spirit's place
now we're together face to face

a heart connection that's unexplained
eye to eye sharing love and pain

different languages when out of the blue
we know each other in moments true

tears glistening hearts open wide
we come together with nothing to hide

i can still feel you tho' the face slipped away
the connection as clear as on that day

in that moment suspended in time
we celebrated a universal divine

A veteran's way

a flag waves
crowds go by
does anyone see
the veteran cry?

perhaps there are no tears
only a vacant stare
screaming memories
of being over there

names on a wall
bronze soldiers raise a flag
or simply a row
of body bags

protecting us
is still what they do
the proud
and the few

tell them you're grateful
that they served
so our flag flies free
our way of life's preserved

Christmas stockings

These stockings are special they come from mom-mom and I;
the love they hold will bring a tear to your eye.

Her bright red wool shirt she had for 586 moons
worn when we camped thru' drought and monsoon.

But now she's gone yet gave her OK
to cut it up and send it your way.

Dad & I worked hard to create a lifetime gift
that will bridge the generations rift.

The scrabble board letters which spell out each name a
adding the history from a family played game.

Each year from now on, a new button I'll add
a special reminder of the year you had.

So these stocking will grow to reflect your living
Mommom, Dad and I will keep on giving – our love.

Truths

it's true
the rabbit died
a wee small babe
is growing inside

small as an almond
he's already made
your life takes a spin
as your old life fades

now it's about
more than you two
responsible for a baby
is scary that's true

where will he sleep?
how to make room
for all the stuff
he'll need so soon

how to teach him
to be patient and kind;
honest and caring
to use his own mind?

you know he'll depend
on you 'til **you** die
it's the scariest of all
i cannot deny

but in there somewhere
is a story untold
of the magic he'll bring
as his life unfolds

take heart my child
as your thoughts take flight
and you get overwhelmed
in the middle of the night

this babe's chosen you
it's his time to be
love taking form
that you can hold and see

Any name will do

call me granny
call me me-maw
i really don't
care at all

what i'd like
to hear you say
"will you please
come and play"

for we will have
so much fun
living each day
on the run

exciting things
to see and do
skipping and laughing
just me and you

Heart shaped shells

perhaps a collage
i will make
out of the heart shells
that i take

i look for perfection
and settle for less
if the shape is sorta close
it's OK, i guess

looking inward
i see my part
seeking perfection
in my own heart

Mom's gone

It has been so long since you were here
and still you're part of all this child holds dear.

In those weeks before you died, I'd hold your hand late at night
we talk of death and how it was done - as you'd fret about doing it right.

Now, you talk to me in unseen ways,
to lighten my load, to brighten my days.

I remember when God took you home to your own mom,
in her beautiful garden of flowers; a world bright and calm.

I feel you beside me, your hand in mine
love light settles in a deep sigh, all is fine.

But the memory that's golden for me is when you stood alone on your feet
and with a connection to my soul, simply told me, "I LOVE YOU"; it was then that I was complete.

How can this be - you're gone while I'm still here
motherless, no one's child and alone with every fear.

But from that day 'til now when I get sad or scared
I remember your words and know you truly cared.

Those three little words carry me through
the living of life a golden gift from you.

The year marched on special days flew by
each one an anniversary to again say goodbye.

It still seems strange you're now in heaven's care;
I can't touch you yet you're everywhere.

Foam

Why it is that when the foamy part of an ocean's wave touches shore, it is soft and caressing on feet and hands?

It's as if after the wave releases its energy only gentleness is left. Fragile and fleeting it is soaked up by the sand. The foam is there for all to freely enjoy.

Infinite grace

down memory lane my heart wanders
seeing those who've gone into the wild blue yonder

with a wing and a prayer they touch in with me
gathering around whispering lovingly

"remember, dear, all is well
you're just right and doing swell"

don't worry 'bout tomorrow you're in good hands
we are keeping watch no matter where you land

you are great and we are proud of you
never giving up - you're right on cue

joy and beauty provide the spark
that will free you from the dark

for you will know both and find balance therein
to fulfill your life before beginning again

we're never far as we wait for you here
until our reunion, you are perfect my dear

remember you are a child of infinite grace
to create as you please, your very own place

love's the only way to be present NOW
we'll lead you home in your final hour

Good enough

it scares me
am i enough
my heart trembles
can i be tough

to stretch and accept
that i am good enough
to make my way
when life gets rough

am i but a grain of sand
battered by heavy tides
or am i good enough
to weather life's ride

not good enough
was my script
seven decades later
i don't give a shit

i yam what i yam
the cartoon would say
i do the best i can
on any given day

i'm very fortunate
to not really care
'cause if i look in a mirror
what i judge is only there

The brothers' bond

they were so young
and off to war
to stop an enemy
on a far away shore

on d-day
they fought for a hold
the brave and scared
they had to be bold

with death and dying
all around
they kept coming
for solid ground

it was a job
that had to be done
doing what they must
the brothers, they won

one side fought
for control and power
the other side responded
protecting freedom's bower

so formed a
true bond of brothers
that fear, filth and gore
are known by no others

survival was a crap shoot
a matter of chance
a buddy beside you
gone in a glance

leaders came and went
for a core of the strong
who held their positions
on a bulge gone wrong

frozen toes
no place warm
keep up morale
for this war's storm

the dead or wounded
never left behind
for those long years
survival was a grind

hedgerows
and fox holes
were covers and blinds
for many lost souls

the long, brutal road
many would question
why are we here
led to frustration

then one day
they finally saw
a concentration camp
and hatred's flaw

the enemy too
drafted their young men
to follow their country
without knowing the end

finally, the enemy
was a subdued race
they could be seen
face to face

they were so alike
sharing the fear and gore
a brotherly bond formed
from a foreign shore

they started with so many
and were whittled down
to the few that were
above ground

each side lost
more than a war
as many young lives
were no more

the bond of brothers
tried and true
secured freedom
for me and you

they remember heroes
with whom they fought
their part wasn't special
to just do what they ought

white crosses a testament
to the sacrifice
of those young soldiers
who never fulfilled life

still today families & nations
celebrate or mourn
those dead and alive
when the brothers were born

About the author

As a military child and then as a military wife, Betty has traveled far and wide. At age 15, she met Bud, who is the love of her life and after more than 52 years of marriage, two kids, seven dogs, eight cats, and a pet rat, she is still living life at 100% and enjoying every moment.

During her childhood, her family moved more than 36 times in 18 years at the whim of the military. These moves introduced her to different cultures, experiences and lives all adding to the richness that is now her life. As a military spouse during Vietnam, she raised her children with grace, beauty and dignity few could imagine during a time of such chaos. Throughout it all, her passion and commitment to the USA, its military and her community stayed strong.

Now, retired in Florida, Betty is living life on her terms and embraces each and every encounter as part of her soul's journey. Having never met a stranger, she invites you into her world of friends and experiences. This collection of poetry serves as a guide to her life experiences from a child of WWII to the challenges of getting older.

She would love to hear from you! You may contact her at
Betty@FieldTripForTheSoul.com or
www.FieldTripForTheSoul.com

List of Poems by Name

Poem Name	Category	Pg
A black hole	Aging/Transition	67
A family of mutts	Family of Fur	83
A good night's sleep	Aging/Transition	34
A monk's singing bowl	Earth/Spirituality	19
A new day	Family/Friends	66
A new life	Family/Friends	77
A new phone	Family/Friends	37
A small glimpse	Family of Fur	58
A space of my own	Passion	63
A veteran's way	Military	85
Acceptance	Aging/Transition	8
Ageless love	Passion	31
All I can do	Aging/Transition	21
Alone	Aging/Transition	32
Am I old yet?	Earth/Spirituality	53
Any name will do	Family/Friends	88
Aunt Ruth	Aging/Transition	18
Being here	Earth/Spirituality	54
By the sea	Earth/Spirituality	50
Captain of my ship	Earth/Spirituality	25
Christmas stockings	Family/Friends	86
Day is done	Aging/Transition	70
Day of water	Earth/Spirituality	79
Days fly by	Earth/Spirituality	29
Dear baby	Family/Friends	81
Do you see me?	Military	56
Earthbound	Military	76
Every five minutes	Family/Friends	14
Field of green	Earth/Spirituality	4
Foam	Earth/Spirituality	91
Friendship	Family/Friends	39
Furious love	Passion	6
Goddesses are we all	Family/Friends	69
Goddesses gather	Family/Friends	49
Good enough	Earth/Spirituality	93
Gratitude	Earth/Spirituality	36
Gray day	Earth/Spirituality	59
Heart shaped shells	Earth/Spirituality	89
Here today	Earth/Spirituality	52
Hiding me	Aging/Transition	51
Homecoming	Family/Friends	47
I already know you	Family/Friends	7
I believe	Earth/Spirituality	24
I'll be there	Family/Friends	16
In the past	Earth/Spirituality	72
Infinite grace	Earth/Spirituality	92
Knowing	Earth/Spirituality	13
Life	Aging/Transition	17
Light and shadow	Earth/Spirituality	57
Little Bit	Family of Fur	9
Looking back	Family/Friends	71
Love	Earth/Spirituality	82
Marriage glue	Family/Friends	74
Mom's gone	Aging/Transition	90
Mommom	Family/Friends	73
Morphing	Aging/Transition	65
My choice	Earth/Spirituality	43
My flag	Military	61
My granddaughter	Family/Friends	11
My mom	Family/Friends	26
My part in the universe	Earth/Spirituality	68
My past	Aging/Transition	38
Ode to my friends	Family/Friends	28
Old scripts	Family/Friends	30
On the road	Passion	75
One day at a time	Aging/Transition	48
Onions	Earth/Spirituality	41
Our feral cat	Family of Fur	60
Pelicans	Earth/Spirituality	22
Places to go and people to see	Earth/Spirituality	84
Princess Peggy	Family/Friends	20
Ryan	Aging/Transition	44
Sauter's farm	Family/Friends	78
Sea	Family/Friends	12
Seen or unseen	Earth/Spirituality	27
Should-ing on myself	Earth/Spirituality	55
Soaring on wings	Earth/Spirituality	45
Straight lines	Family/Friends	35
The brothers' bond	Military	94
The USAF dad	Military	62
Things	Family/Friends	15
Ticking clock	Earth/Spirituality	33
Time	Earth/Spirituality	64
Travel companion	Aging/Transition	46
Traveling with pop	Military	10
Truths	Family/Friends	87
Trying to nap	Passion	40
Where does sound end?	Earth/Spirituality	42
Which direction is the right direction	Aging/Transition	23
Young love	Passion	80

List of Poems by Page Number

Poem Name	Category	Pg
Field of green	Earth/Spirituality	4
Furious love	Passion	6
I already know you	Family/Friends	7
Acceptance	Aging/Transition	8
Little Bit	Family of Fur	9
Traveling with pop	Military	10
My granddaughter	Family/Friends	11
Sea	Family/Friends	12
Knowing	Earth/Spirituality	13
Every five minutes	Family/Friends	14
Things	Family/Friends	15
I'll be there	Family/Friends	16
Life	Aging/Transition	17
Aunt Ruth	Aging/Transition	18
A monk's singing bowl	Earth/Spirituality	19
Princess Peggy	Family/Friends	20
All I can do	Aging/Transition	21
Pelicans	Earth/Spirituality	22
Which direction is the right direction	Aging/Transition	23
I believe	Earth/Spirituality	24
Captain of my ship	Earth/Spirituality	25
My mom	Family/Friends	26
Seen or unseen	Earth/Spirituality	27
Ode to my friends	Family/Friends	28
Days fly by	Earth/Spirituality	29
Old scripts	Family/Friends	30
Ageless love	Passion	31
Alone	Aging/Transition	32
Ticking clock	Earth/Spirituality	33
A good night's sleep	Aging/Transition	34
Straight lines	Family/Friends	35
Gratitude	Earth/Spirituality	36
A new phone	Family/Friends	37
My past	Aging/Transition	38
Friendship	Family/Friends	39
Trying to nap	Passion	40
Onions	Earth/Spirituality	41
Where does sound end?	Earth/Spirituality	42
My choice	Earth/Spirituality	43
Ryan	Aging/Transition	44
Soaring on wings	Earth/Spirituality	45
Travel companion	Aging/Transition	46
Homecoming	Family/Friends	47
One day at a time	Aging/Transition	48
Goddesses gather	Family/Friends	49
By the sea	Earth/Spirituality	50
Hiding me	Aging/Transition	51
Here today	Earth/Spirituality	52
Am I old yet?	Earth/Spirituality	53
Being here	Earth/Spirituality	54
Should-ing on myself	Earth/Spirituality	55
Do you see me?	Military	56
Light and shadow	Earth/Spirituality	57
A small glimpse	Family of Fur	58
Gray day	Earth/Spirituality	59
Our feral cat	Family of Fur	60
My flag	Military	61
The USAF dad	Military	62
A space of my own	Passion	63
Time	Earth/Spirituality	64
Morphing	Aging/Transition	65
A new day	Family/Friends	66
A black hole	Aging/Transition	67
My part in the universe	Earth/Spirituality	68
Goddesses are we all	Family/Friends	69
Day is done	Aging/Transition	70
Looking back	Family/Friends	71
In the past	Earth/Spirituality	72
Mommom	Family/Friends	73
Marriage glue	Family/Friends	74
On the road	Passion	75
Earthbound	Military	76
A new life	Family/Friends	77
Sauter's farm	Family/Friends	78
Day of water	Earth/Spirituality	79
Young love	Passion	80
Dear baby	Family/Friends	81
Love	Earth/Spirituality	82
A family of mutts	Family of Fur	83
Places to go and people to see	Earth/Spirituality	84
A veteran's way	Military	85
Christmas stockings	Family/Friends	86
Truths	Family/Friends	87
Any name will do	Family/Friends	88
Heart shaped shells	Earth/Spirituality	89
Mom's gone	Aging/Transition	90
Foam	Earth/Spirituality	91
Infinite grace	Earth/Spirituality	92
Good enough	Earth/Spirituality	93
The brothers' bond	Military	94